Barry Sanders

Additional titles in the Sports Reports *series:*

Michael Jordan
Star Guard
(0-89490-482-5)

Jim Kelly
Star Quarterback
(0-89490-446-9)

Chris Mullin
Star Forward
(0-89490-486-8)

Cal Ripken, Jr.
Star Shortstop
(0-89490-485-X)

David Robinson
Star Center
(0-89490-483-3)

Barry Sanders
Star Running Back
(0-89490-484-1)

Thurman Thomas
Star Running Back
(0-89490-445-0)

SPORTS REPORTS

Barry Sanders

Star Running Back

Nathan Aaseng

ENSLOW PUBLISHERS, INC.

Bloy St. & Ramsey Ave.	P. O. Box 38
Box 777	Aldershot
Hillside, N.J. 07205	Hants GU12 6BP
U.S.A.	U.K.

Library of Congress Cataloging-in-Publication Data

Aaseng, Nathan.
    Barry Sanders: Star running back / Nathan Aaseng.
       p. cm. — (Sport reports)
    Includes bibliographical references (p.) and index.
    ISBN 0-89490-484-1
    1. Sanders, Barry, 1966–   —Juvenile literature. 2. Football
players—United States—Biography—Juvenile literature. I. Title.
II. Series.
GV939.S18A27 1994
796.332'092—dc20
   [B]   93-6173
                                                 CIP
                                                AC

Printed in the United States of America

10 9 8 7 6 5 4 3 2 1

Photo Credits: Jonathan Daniel, Courtesy of Northwestern University, p.
20; Detroit Lions, pp. 8, 53; Evanston Photo Studios, Courtesy of Northwestern University, p. 18; Courtesy of Oklahoma State University, pp. 23,
26, 31, 32, 33; Rick Orndorf, pp. 14, 45, 47, 57, 69, 70, 74, 79, 81, 84, 91, 92.

Cover Photo: Vernon Biever

Contents

Chapter 1

"Let's Win It and Go Home"

The University of Wyoming Cowboys trotted out for their pregame warmups. They were eager to get a close look at the little running back who would be playing against them. Few of the Wyoming football players had ever seen Barry Sanders perform, even on television.

They were not alone. Most of the fans entering the stadium for the 1988 Holiday Bowl had seen little of Sanders other than on highlight clips. Sanders had not been actively recruited out of high school. He played for Oklahoma State University, a school that lived in the long football shadow cast by its cross-state rival—the University of Oklahoma. The Oklahoma State Cowboys were better known for wrestling than for football, and as a result few of their games were televised.

Sanders had burst upon the college scene with

Barry Sanders

little warning. Prior to this season, he had made some electrifying runs as a kick returner. But he had been only a second-string running back. Given a chance to start as a junior, he had shattered 34 major college football records. Sanders had accomplished this feat without showing off. The serious young man never strutted or celebrated on the field. He never danced in the end zone, never even spiked the ball after a touchdown run. In fact, Sanders ducked the spotlight every chance he could. As quietly as possible, he had become college football's most exciting player.

The Wyoming team was primed to put Sanders to the test. They had breezed through their schedule with 10 wins and only one loss, slightly better than Oklahoma State's 9–2 mark. This nationally televised Holiday Bowl would let a large audience see whether Barry Sanders could live up to his press clippings.

· Sanders did not keep the Wyoming team or the curious fans waiting long. On Oklahoma State's first offensive series, he rocketed through a hole in the defensive line. The Wyoming team barely laid a hand on him. Sanders sprinted 33 yards for a touchdown, and with a successful conversion, Oklahoma State led 7–0.

Little number 21 was held in check for a time

after that. Oklahoma State was not able to mount another serious threat until near the end of the half. Sanders capped this drive with a two-yard touchdown burst. When the point after was successfully kicked his team had a 14–0 lead.

Wyoming hovered within striking distance early in the second half. But with the score 24–10 in favor of Oklahoma State, Sanders took over the contest. In the third quarter he raced 67 yards for one touchdown, ran one yard for another, and scampered 10 yards for yet another score.

Sanders's scoring frenzy padded Oklahoma State's lead to 45–14. Wyoming coach Paul Roach had seen all he needed to see. "Barry Sanders was everything that he was advertised," said Roach[1]. Sanders had gained 229 yards in only 29 carries and had scored five touchdowns. To top it all off, he had completed a 17-yard pass, the first of his career.

With the game well under control, Oklahoma State prepared to send in their reserves. But at the start of the fourth quarter, someone noticed that Sanders was close to a record. His 229 yards were only three shy of the Holiday Bowl rushing mark of 232 yards. Oklahoma State coach Pat Jones explained to Sanders how close he was to the record. He asked if Sanders wanted to go back in and claim his bit of glory.

"I'd rather not," Sanders said simply.[2] The game was won; he had done his job. Records and statistics just did not excite him.

The Holiday Bowl showed football fans that Barry Sanders was the real thing. His lightning-quick moves and explosive power proved he could play running back as well as the position has ever been

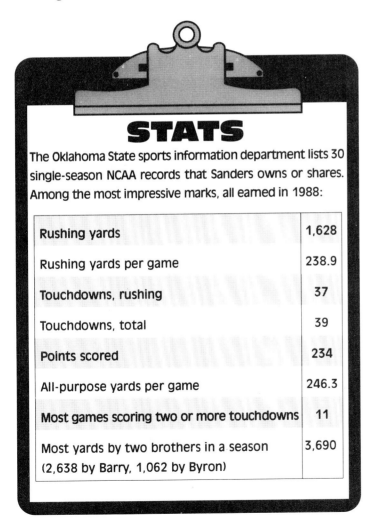

STATS

The Oklahoma State sports information department lists 30 single-season NCAA records that Sanders owns or shares. Among the most impressive marks, all earned in 1988:

Rushing yards	1,628
Rushing yards per game	238.9
Touchdowns, rushing	37
Touchdowns, total	39
Points scored	234
All-purpose yards per game	246.3
Most games scoring two or more touchdowns	11
Most yards by two brothers in a season (2,638 by Barry, 1,062 by Byron)	3,690

played. And he did not need headlines and records to pump him up. Sanders knew who he was and what he was about.

A year later he showed that a $2 million contract and a brilliant rookie season as a pro had not changed him a bit. In the final game of the season, Sanders ripped through the Atlanta Falcons with ease. He racked up 158 yards in 20 carries, including touchdown runs of 25, 17, and 18 yards. With one minute to go, his Detroit Lions had the ball and a 31–24 lead. A few basic plays would use up the clock and give them their fifth straight victory.

Sanders was sitting on the bench, watching the reserves finish up the game. Lions' officials, however, discovered that Barry's season rushing total stood at 1,470 yards. They told Coach Wayne Fontes that Kansas City's thundering fullback, Christian Okoye, had finished his final game of the season with 1,480 yards. If Sanders could collect just 11 more yards, he would capture the NFL's rushing title. That would be a proud achievement, especially for a rookie. Sanders' name would be etched in the record books alongside the greatest pro runners of all time.

At the rate he had been tearing through the Falcons, Sanders would need only one or two carries to pick up those 11 yards. Fontes asked Barry if he wanted to go back in the game to get the rushing title.

The rookie running back was not even tempted. "Coach, let's just win it and go home," he said.[3]

Barry Sanders knows who he is. He knows that football is a team sport. He would be the first to say that a running back cannot gain any yards or win games without teammates. He believes that a good player places team goals ahead of individual glory.

Barry Sanders also knows that teamwork is important in life. He believes that what he accomplishes off the field is more important than the feats he performs between the chalk lines. "If I couldn't play football," he reminds fans, "I'd still be the same person with the same convictions."[4] Defensive back William White speaks for the rest of the Lions when he says that Barry "lives the life that he's portraying. His actions speak so loud you don't need to hear what he's saying."[5]

To a man, the Detroit Lions believe that Barry Sanders is a very special person. During Barry's rookie year, veteran placekicker Eddie Murray said of the 21-year-old Sanders, "He's light years ahead of most people in the league his age in maturity."[6]

Sanders bristles at the idea that he is anything special. He will tell you that football is just a game and a job. Sure, he is good at his job. But then so are many other people who do not get as much publicity. "I try to make people understand that I'm really not that much different than anybody else. I'm one of 11 kids and I had a very normal life."[7]

With apologies to Barry Sanders, those who have seen him play football will insist that Sanders

Seeing his path blocked, Sanders screeches to a halt and changes directions in a flash.

is one of a kind. Rival defensive lineman Trace Armstrong of the Chicago Bears says, "He's like a little sports car. He can stop on a dime and go from zero to 60 in seconds."[8] Former Buffalo Bills' general manager Bill Polian and Minnesota Vikings' defensive coordinator Tony Dungy made identical statements when commenting on Sanders: "You gotta hold your breath every time he touches the ball."[9]

No matter how Barry tries to shrug off publicity, it keeps following him around. People keep marveling and gasping and shaking their heads at Sanders' slippery, body-bending moves. But no matter how people admire him, Sanders just responds the way he has done all along. He ignores the praise and goes on with his life as the same humble kid who grew up in Wichita, Kansas.

Chapter 2

Too Small

Barry Sanders was born on July 16, 1968, in Wichita, Kansas, a city of more than a quarter of a million people in the middle of the western plain. He was the seventh child of William and Shirley Sanders, who were already raising two boys and four girls by the time Barry came along. Four more girls were to follow.

William Sanders had lived all his life in a poor section of Wichita. He worked as a carpenter and a roofer to support his growing family. No matter how hard William tried, though, his income barely managed to pay the basic bills.

Barry's parents were sometimes discouraged by their difficult conditions. But they were determined to provide the support, guidance, and love that their children needed. William was a loud, talkative person who provided firm discipline in his outspoken way. "My dad always shot straight," remembers Barry. "He didn't beat around the bush."[1]

Shirley's special gift to the family was her caring manner and her strong religious beliefs. She stayed home to be with the children while they were growing up. Only after the youngest was raised did Shirley attend Wichita State University to earn a nursing degree. While the children were young, "she took us to church every Sunday," according to Barry.[2] All the Sanders children attended the Vacation Bible School that Shirley helped lead at Paradise Baptist Church.

The Sanders boys, especially, needed all the care and attention that their parents could provide to keep them in line. The oldest, Boyd, had a troubled childhood. The younger two, Byron and Barry, sometimes strayed into mischief.

"When I was younger, people thought I was a bully," says Barry. "I got into fights and did a lot of wrong."[3] Byron and Barry stole candy. They started a fire on the floor of their bathroom. They were even arrested for trespassing.

Once youngsters start making bad choices, minor mistakes can snowball into serious trouble. Barry sometimes wonders how close he came to getting mixed up with the wrong crowd. But the

Byron Sanders, the older brother with whom Barry shared many childhood adventures.

close-knit family bond and religious training held fast. Boyd, whom Barry admired greatly, settled down to become a minister. Barry's life seemed headed in a similar direction. The Sanders' pastor at Paradise Baptist, Rev. Paul L. Gray, Sr., remembers Barry as "being all boy, but having a genuine concern about the Lord from an early age."[4]

Byron and Barry also became involved in sports, particularly football. Barry's gift for running with a football started to show when he was in the fourth grade. But over the next few years, his speed and ability to shift direction were outweighed by a glaring problem. Barry seemed to be too small to play such a rugged sport. That problem was one that would haunt him all the way to the National Football League (NFL).

"Other kids had a growth spurt before me," says Sanders. By the time he reached the ninth grade, Barry still stood only five feet tall and barely tipped the scales at 100 pounds.[5] Coaches kept him on the sidelines and out of harm's way throughout most of the football season. "It's amazing how much coaches pay attention to size," Barry says.[6]

At that point, no one had any reason to imagine that little Barry might ever be a football star. But Sanders liked the game. He refused to be discouraged by his lack of playing time. He was determined to make up for his size with quickness and hustle. Even as he sat on the bench, he dreamed of someday playing college football.

Barry finally did grow—some. He reached five feet seven inches and about 155 pounds by his junior year. He had learned to use his quickness to good advantage. Although still one of the shortest players on the field, he showed excellent athletic talent. Barry also made the varsity team in basketball, a sport in which size is even more important.

Barry's fierce desire to succeed was further fueled by his brother's football success. Byron was a year ahead of Barry in school. He broke into the Wichita North starting backfield while Barry was still riding the bench. Byron played well enough to receive a football scholarship from Northwestern University. During his senior year at Northwestern, Byron would gain over 1,000 yards rushing. But while in high school, he nearly cost Barry a chance for a scholarship of his own. With Byron holding down the starting tailback spot through his senior year, Barry rarely got a chance to run the ball.

His interest in football jolted him out of some lazy habits in the classroom. Barry had not been a good student in his early years. But he soon discovered that there was a price to be paid if he failed to

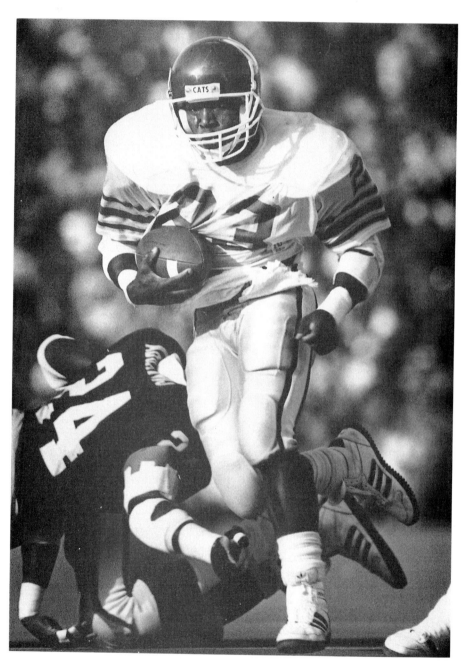

Byron, running for Northwestern, shares a national collegiate record for most yards gained by brothers in a season. Byron rushed for 1,062 yards in 1988.

buckle down to his studies. "I had to learn to be a student athlete because I couldn't play if my grades fell," he said later.[7]

As Barry started his senior season at Wichita North in 1985, his dream of playing major college football seemed like wishful thinking. His coaches seemed to wonder if he were big enough to succeed at such a tough game even on the high school level. They toyed with the idea of making him a pass receiver. Playing that position, he would not have to slam into those huge linemen.

Barry started off his senior year as a receiver. Not until only five games remained in the season did Barry finally get his chance to start at running back.

Sanders made the most of his opportunity. His speed and his waterbug moves left tacklers grasping at air and gasping for breath. Barry led the team in kickoff returns and in rushing during his senior year. Despite his late start as a runner, he finished the year as the second-leading rusher in the city. He was even named to some honorable mention All-State teams.

Barry hoped his success would catch the attention of college recruiters, who were combing the country in search of football talent. His dad especially hoped that his favorite team, the University of Oklahoma, would come calling for Barry.

But Oklahoma never called. In fact, few college coaches were impressed with Sanders. Barry's team had not won very many games. Barry had performed well but had not done anything spectacular. A few college recruiters checked Barry out. But as soon as they saw his size, they moved on to look at more promising prospects. A five-foot eight-inch, 170-pound running back could do all right in high school but would have a rough time of it on the college level.

Barry's coaches tried to help him by putting together a highlight film of his season. The University of Nebraska simply sent the film back without viewing it. One major college recruiter who was working in the Wichita area admits, "We didn't even look at him."[8]

One school that did view his highlight film was Oklahoma State, which did not have nearly the football reputation of the University of Oklahoma. But its program had improved in recent years. Barry's highlight film persuaded the Oklahoma State coaches to offer him a scholarship. But even they had modest hopes for him.

"Frankly," said OSU's head coach, Pat Jones, "he wasn't a big name on our board. We thought he could play for us but we weren't pursuing him that heavily."[9]

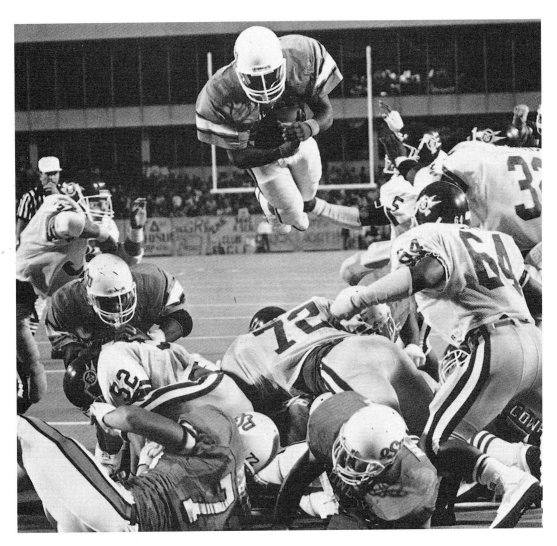

All American Thurman Thomas had the starting tailback position nailed down at Oklahoma State when Sanders arrived. Barry could only watch and learn as Thomas helped the Cowboys soar to new heights.

Fortunately for OSU, no one else was pursuing him heavily, either. The only other Division I school to offer Sanders a football scholarship was Wichita State. Barry's hometown school was hardly a major football power. Sanders chose Oklahoma State even though he knew that meant at least two more years of riding the bench. The Cowboys' running attack was spearheaded by none other than Thurman Thomas. Pro scouts considered Thomas a top prospect. As a sophomore in 1985, he had finished fourth in the nation in rushing. No newcomer had a chance to bump Thomas out of the starting lineup—especially not an undersized freshman who had started only five games in his high school career.

As luck would have it, Thomas injured his knee playing basketball with friends the summer before Sanders enrolled at OSU. Thomas was forced to sit out a large part of Barry's freshman season. The "two-small" Sanders took advantage of Thomas's absence to get into a few games. He rushed 25 times for 132 yards and a touchdown against Illinois State. He carried the ball 22 times for 86 yards and a touchdown against Missouri. Oklahoma State also called on Barry to return punts and kickoffs in three games.

But even with Thomas out of the lineup, Barry

spent most of the year on the bench. Outside of the Illinois State and Missouri games, Barry rushed only 27 times all year.

While biding his time as benchwarmer and part-time player at college, Barry continued to build up his strength. He also focused on his studies to prepare himself for a career after he graduated. "If I'm going to spend the time doing it, I might as well get something out of it," he decided.[10] Rather than coast along doing the minimum, Sanders signed up for tough course loads. His main interest was business management, economics, and accounting.

Thurman Thomas returned healthy for his senior year in 1987. But at the same time, Coach Jones began to recognize Sanders' talents as an open-field runner. He assigned Barry the full-time job of returning kickoffs and punts. The sophomore instantly rewarded Jones's faith. On the Cowboys' first kickoff return of the 1987 season, Sanders caught the ball at the goal line and rocketed upfield. Leaving Tulsa University defenders in his wake, he sped 100 yards for a touchdown.

As Sanders' ability became obvious, Coach Jones tried to squeeze in some more playing time for him. Sanders made the most of his limited role as Thomas's backup. He gained 92 yards in only nine carries against Wyoming. He stunned powerful

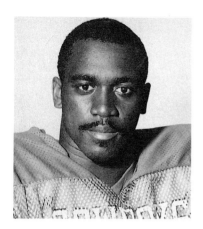

When Thurman Thomas was drafted by the Bills in 1987, Sanders got his chance at a starting position.

Nebraska by racking up 60 yards in just seven carries. Coach Jones kept rewarding Sanders with more and more playing time. Near the end of the season, Barry picked up 105 yards rushing against Kansas State, 116 against Kansas, and 122 against Iowa State.

Meanwhile, Sanders led the nation in kickoff returns with an average of 31.3 yards per return. He also scored on a breathtaking 68-yard punt return against Houston and a 73-yard punt return against Colorado.

Such performances might have attracted a great deal of acclaim at most schools. But Oklahoma State was still the home of Thurman Thomas. Fully recovered from his knee injury, the senior running back scampered for 1,613 yards, the third highest rushing total among NCAA large schools. He earned recognition as the Big Eight Conference's 1987 Player of the Year. Thomas finished his career as the second leading rusher in Big Eight history.

Sanders was simply stuck in the background until Thomas finished his college career. Thomas would go on to prove his worth as a pro player. A second-round selection of the Buffalo Bills in the 1987 NFL draft, he quickly became pro football's top all-purpose running back.

With Thomas gone, Sanders finally had a fighting

chance to get into the starting lineup in 1988. But even his spectacular showing as a kick returner and reserve runner did not erase the doubts caused by his size. When asked to comment on his team for the upcoming 1988 season, Coach Jones did not consider Sanders a certain starter. He indicated that Sanders would probably share the position with Mitch Nash. Jones expected good things from both of them. "Those two together will have about the same statistics as Thomas," Jones predicted.[11]

That was a bold claim considering they were filling the shoes of the best player in OSU history. But Sanders had grown used to being downgraded because of his size. He looked forward to the chance to prove to the doubters that height and weight are not the only things that count. He especially relished a chance to play against some of those Big Eight Conference schools that had made the mistake of writing him off.

Chapter 3

The Unknown Superstar

The Oklahoma State football staff figured that their 1988 team would field one of the most powerful offenses in school history. Quarterback Mike Gundy was a strong leader and an accurate passer. His main target, flashy Hart Lee Dykes, had already made his mark as one of the most exciting wide receivers in the game. A veteran, all-senior offensive line would provide solid pass protection and run-blocking. Cary Blanchard was one of the most accurate place-kickers in the country.

But Barry Sanders wasted no time in showing that he would be the star of the show. Playing against Miami University (Ohio), Barry stood at the goal line for the first kickoff of the season. In an instant replay of the previous year, Barry caught the ball and dashed forward into the chaos of 21 flying bodies. In a split second he saw the opening and burst through it. Once Sanders broke into the clear, no one could catch him. He became the first player in NCAA football history to return a season-opening kickoff for a touchdown two years in a row.

There was no more talk about Sanders sharing the tailback spot with anyone. "He just takes your breath away," Jones marveled.[1]

Before long Sanders had a great many opponents heading for the oxygen masks. Little Barry Sanders started off solidly with 178 yards and two touchdowns against Miami (Ohio), then 157 yards and two touchdowns against Texas A & M. He captured national headlines for the first time with 310 yards and five touchdowns against Tulsa. Proving that was no fluke, he crossed the end zone four more times against Colorado.

There were still those who questioned whether Sanders could do anything against a top college team. It is one thing to run wild against Tulsa and Miami (Ohio). However, it was a far different matter to do the same against Nebraska and Oklahoma.

But Barry got a measure of revenge against Nebraska. Carrying the bulk of the offensive load against the Cornhuskers, Sanders rushed 35 times for 189 yards and four more touchdowns. After an unspectacular performance against Missouri, Sanders ran wild against Kansas State. He slashed through the Wildcats for 320 yards and three touchdowns.

That brought him up against Oklahoma, the team his dad had hoped would recruit him. By this time, Sanders had gained a big reputation in the Big Eight Conference. The highly rated Sooners were geared to stop him. This game, broadcast on ESPN, would also give many fans their first and only look at Sanders during the regular season. Sanders ran the ball tirelessly and nearly beat the Sooners by himself. He gained 215 yards in 39 carries, scored two touchdowns, and caught two more passes for 30 yards. The Cowboys came within an eyelash of upsetting the Sooners, but lost 24–21.

From that point on, Sanders was like a brush fire out of control. He burned Kansas for 312 yards and five touchdowns and then scorched Iowa State for 293 yards and four touchdowns.

By this time, Sanders was no longer just "the best player you've never heard of," as *Sports Illustrated* had described him earlier in the season.[2] Oklahoma coach Barry Switzer declared Sanders to be "the best college player in America."[3]

Sanders had proved the skeptics wrong. That put him in a good position to gloat and bask in the glow of his success. But that was not Barry's way.

Sanders simply ran with the ball, dazzled the crowds, and then quietly went about his business.

Reporters trying to get interesting quotes from the new star were frustrated. Sanders was not interested in talking about himself. "I try to study and stay out of trouble," he said.[4] When he did comment on a game, he usually talked about his offensive line. They were the ones who were making him look good, he insisted.

Sanders squirts through a hole in Nebraska's defense.

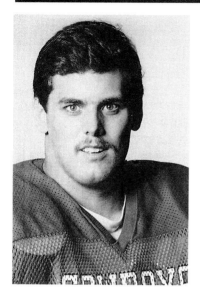

This man's autograph is in Barry's collection. Sanders appreciates his blockers, such as Oklahoma State teammate Jason Kidder.

Cowboy lineman Jason Kidder found out that Sanders' modesty was not just an act for the press. "The other day, Barry asked *me* for *my* autograph," Kidder reported, astounded. "I asked why and he said, 'Because I'm not better than you are.'"[5]

Sanders recognized that sudden fame and fortune bring temptations to young athletes. Some players get carried away by all the praise. They become arrogant and take advantage of their fame. Sanders was determined that this would not happen to him. Once when he was filling up his gas tank in Oklahoma City, the station manager recognized him as a football star. The manager tried to slip Barry some money as a reward for his efforts at OSU.

Although Sanders did not have much money at the time, he refused to take it. He knew that college athletes are not supposed to accept money, and he would not break the rules. He would wait until he turned pro to earn his money.

This dizzying new world of fame bothered the quiet Sanders. More and more, he came to believe that his religious upbringing held the key to inner peace. Although most people would have considered him an admirable person, Sanders was worried about himself.

"By man's standards I probably wasn't doing

anything really bad. But we are judged by God," he said. "I knew I had to change. My junior year in college, I really, really made a change."[6]

"His attendance to the Wednesday night Bible Study when home from his college is what cemented this young man into my memory," recalls his pastor, Rev. Gray.[7]

While Barry was trying to get his life in order, his football success was nearly burning out the calculators at OSU. Sanders had more than made good on Coach Jones's prediction that the Cowboy backfield could equal the numbers put up by Thurman Thomas. In just the first ten games of the season, Sanders shattered Thomas's team rushing mark by nearly half a mile!

The Cowboys posted an 8–2 record going into their final regular season contest against Texas Tech. Enthusiastic Japanese fans of American football had arranged that this game would be played in Japan. Many of the Oklahoma State players wanted to take advantage of this rare chance to visit a foreign country. Sanders declined at least one invitation to go sightseeing, though, in order to get caught up on his studies.

By this time, Sanders had become the favorite to win the Heisman Trophy. This award is given each year to the top college football player. The winner

The Heisman hoopla had little effect on Barry. He was more interested in getting caught up on his homework than in posing for pictures such as this.

of the award was due to be announced the very day of the Oklahoma State-Texas Tech contest. The television network that carried the awards show was certain that Sanders would win. They set up a satellite connection so that they could interview Barry live after the award was announced.

Sanders was not interested. He hated awards ceremonies of all kinds. He said that he was not that interested in winning the Heisman Trophy. That had never been one of his goals. He had far more important things on his mind, such as preparing for the game with Texas Tech. "I really don't want to do it," he said about the telecast.[8]

FACT

Barry's spectacular season took the suspense out of the Heisman Trophy voting in 1988. Sanders won in an avalanche over his three closest rivals, all quarterbacks.

PLAYER	COLLEGE	FIRST PLACE VOTES	TOTAL VOTES
1. Barry Sanders	Oklahoma State	559	1,878
2. Rodney Peete	USC	70	912
3. Troy Aikman	UCLA	31	582
4. Steve Walsh	Miami	16	341

The network was shocked. They had a big investment tied up in this award and in the satellite hookup. Under pressure, Sanders finally backed down and agreed to the interview. Sure enough, Barry easily won the award over two quarterbacks, Southern California's Rodney Peete and UCLA's Troy Aikman. Sanders accepted the award graciously. He gave the credit to his teammates and showed no excitement.

Five hours later, the Heisman Trophy winner took the field for the final regular season game of the year. If anyone doubted that Sanders had deserved the award, his performance in that game settled the question of who was the best college player in the United States. In the first quarter, Sanders scampered for 15 yards. That pushed him past the single-season rushing record of 2,342 yards held by Marcus Allen of the University of Southern California. Sanders then soared high over the line to score on a one-yard plunge to stake the Cowboys to an early lead.

Texas Tech struck back to move ahead 14–7 in the second quarter. Sanders answered with a 56-yard touchdown sprint, and soon the score was tied. Texas Tech continued to score almost at will. But they could not stop Sanders. The back who was once considered too small to play college football gave a remarkable demonstration of strength. Sanders carried the ball 42 times for 257 yards. His four touchdowns helped Oklahoma State finally come out on top, 45–42.

Sanders had actually gained yards at such a fast pace that the record keepers could not keep up with him. At first officials reported that Sanders had finished the season with a total of 2,553 yards rushing. That was more than 200 yards over the previous record.

But since the Tokyo Stadium had no press box, the game officials had been placed in the top row of the stands. From that position they had been unable to see well. In reviewing the tapes of the game, record keepers found that two of Sanders' pass catches were actually lateral passes. Lateral passes are not forward passes and so are included in rushing totals.

These two plays tagged another 75 yards onto Sanders' rushing numbers.[9] That gave him over 300 yards rushing in a game for the fourth time. No other player had ever gained that much more than once! Sanders set a new NCAA career mark with 2,628 yards rushing. His record of 238.9 rushing yards per game averaged out to nearly eight yards per carry.

Many small, quick backs have trouble hanging

onto the football, but Sanders fumbled only once in 344 carries. Perhaps the most impressive of the 34 NCAA records that Oklahoma State claimed for Sanders were his totals of 39 touchdowns and 60 more points than had ever been scored by one college player in a season!

When Sanders returned home after the Texas Tech

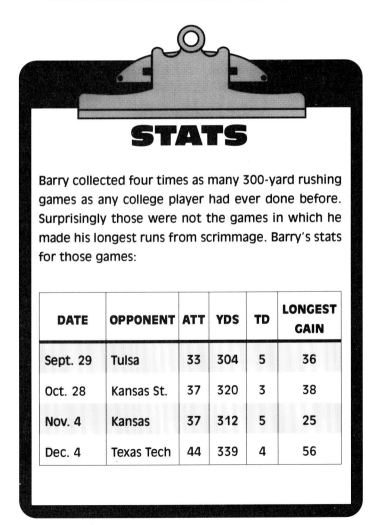

STATS

Barry collected four times as many 300-yard rushing games as any college player had ever done before. Surprisingly those were not the games in which he made his longest runs from scrimmage. Barry's stats for those games:

DATE	OPPONENT	ATT	YDS	TD	LONGEST GAIN
Sept. 29	Tulsa	33	304	5	36
Oct. 28	Kansas St.	37	320	3	38
Nov. 4	Kansas	37	312	5	25
Dec. 4	Texas Tech	44	339	4	56

game, his family rushed to greet him. In contrast to Barry's calm, even nature, William Sanders charged into the room. He hugged his son and wrestled him to the ground in delight. "Everyone at home is proud of you," he said, "but keep trusting in God and don't let things get out of whack."[10]

Sanders did not let things get out of whack even when his talent caught the attention of President-elect George Bush. Fresh from his 1988 election victory, Bush invited Sanders to his presidential inauguration. But Barry was so dedicated to his goals that he would not be distracted even by such an honor. The demands of the football season had put Sanders behind in his studies. All that Heisman fuss, plus the Cowboys' victorious trip to the Holiday Bowl, had made matters worse. Sanders knew he had a multimillion dollar pro football contract in his future. He could easily have decided that he no longer needed to study.

But Barry believed his studies were important. He turned down the president's invitation. According to OSU sports information director Steve Buzzard, "He just didn't feel like he could miss any more class time."[11]

Chapter 4

The Decision

Sanders looked forward to an even better senior season in 1989. But while Oklahoma State was savoring its Holiday Bowl victory, the squad was hit with grim news. The NCAA had found that OSU had broken some rules on recruiting high school players. As punishment, the NCAA placed the Cowboy football program on probation. The result was that none of the team's 1989 games would be televised, and OSU would not be allowed to play in any postseason bowl games.

The blow could not have come at a worse time for Oklahoma State. For the first time, the Cowboys had *the* prime attraction in college football. They would have had more televised games than ever. Now many observers wondered if Sanders would return to college for his final year. He was obviously good enough to jump right to the pros.

Should Barry leave school now and join the pros? The entire Sanders family began to discuss the question. The debate put a strain on the close-knit group.

William Sanders argued strongly Barry should leave college. What if Barry suffered a serious injury in practice or in one of the games of his final year? That would cost him a chance to earn millions. Why take the chance? Also, Oklahoma State's entire offensive line had been seniors the year before. They would not be back. Barry would not get the blocking from the new inexperienced linemen that he had enjoyed during his junior year. His statistics could well drop, and his value might fall as well. William Sanders wanted Barry to sign a contract while he could get good value for his services. "You'd be crazy to go back and play at OSU," William insisted.[1]

Shirley Sanders took the other side. She believed in the value of education. She hoped Barry would stay in college until he got his degree. Football might not pan out. Even if injuries did not cut short his career, few running backs lasted longer than four or five years in the pros. What would Barry do when his career was over if he did not have his college education?

Barry wrestled with both points of view and tried to make up his mind. He wanted to carry out his mom's wish that he finish school. At the same time, he wanted to please his father and earn a huge salary.

Barry's confusion made the debate more intense. His father argued even more strongly. William Sanders had spent a lifetime working hard for little money. He was eager, almost desperate, to be done with that. A pro football contract was the family's one chance to get ahead. "It'll get me off these rooftops and take the hammer out of my hand," he said. Barry's indecision frustrated him. "Get out of school so we can get on with our lives," said William.[2]

Barry's sisters joined their mother's side. They did not like the pressure their father was putting on Barry. They thought Barry should be allowed to make up his own mind about what he wanted to do with his life.

Behind in his studies and with little reason to return to a team on probation, Barry finally settled the issue. He announced that he would leave school and make himself available for the upcoming pro draft.

As the pro scouts took a closer look at him, though, Sanders heard a familiar criticism. It was the same gloomy prediction that had been followed to every level of play. "Sure, Sanders is a good runner, but he's too small!" NFL players were bigger, stronger, and faster than the defenders Sanders had run over in college. Pro coaches liked large, punishing backs. They liked runners who could dish out, as well as take, a pounding. They were also looking for backs who could do more than just run with the ball. Pro teams expected their backs to block and to catch passes. Sanders had done little besides run with the ball at Oklahoma State. In his final season he caught only 19 passes for 106 yards. His coaches had rarely asked him to throw a block.

FACT

Had he played his senior year at OSU, Sanders would undoubtedly have broken many NCAA career records. Even with only one full season as a starter, Sanders set the following career marks:

Most 300-yard rushing games	4
Most consecutive games scoring two or more TDs	13
Most consecutive games rushing for two or more TDs	12

Pro scouts were not always impressed by great college performances. Every year top college stars fell on their faces when they tried to make it in the pros. Terry Baker, John Huarte, Gary Beban, Johnny Rodgers, and Pat Sullivan had all won the Heisman Trophy. But they just were not big enough or fast enough to do well as pros. Sanders seemed to fit the same mold.

A few football experts, though, spotted something special about Barry. Washington Redskins' general manager Bobby Beathard, one of the NFL's top talent judges, believed that Sanders was the kind of player who thrived on new challenges. "Everyone in the Big Eight was pointing for him," Beathard observed. "Yet he consistently had his best games against the best teams."[3]

When draft day arrived, the Dallas Cowboys selected first. They chose strong-armed quarterback Troy Aikman. Green Bay also passed up the chance to get Sanders. They chose massive offensive tackle Tony Mandarich instead. The Detroit Loins were up next.

The Lions needed help at nearly every position. A few weeks earlier, Coach Wayne Fontes had been debating whether to take Sanders with his highest draft pick. Detroit had converted to the new "run-and-shoot" offense that was built almost completely around the passing game. Where would a pure runner like Sanders fit into this attack?

Fontes also questioned whether Sanders was fast enough for the pros. Scouts had not yet had a chance to time Barry in the 40-yard dash. "Of course in all the film we saw, we never saw anyone catch him," Fontes admitted.[4]

Shortly before the draft, Sanders went through some tests for pro scouts. He erased all doubts about his speed with a 4:39 clocking in the 40-yard dash. But the feat that really sold Fontes was Sanders' vertical leap of nearly 42 inches. Some of the most famous leapers and jammers in pro basketball could not jump that high! Fontes realized that Sanders had to be an incredible athlete. The Lions wasted no time in claiming him with that third selection of the draft.

Now it was Sanders' turn to have doubts about the Lions. He knew that the Lions had been one of the NFL's weaker teams for many years. They seldom made the play-offs. They appeared no closer to fielding a champion team now than when they had started rebuilding several years ago. Furthermore, Sanders realized that the run-and-shoot was primarily a passing offense. It was not designed to highlight the skills of a running back. Sanders wondered if he would

FACT

Critics often say that Sanders does not run well on natural grass. They say that his darting changes of direction and lightning acceleration work only on dry artificial turf—such as the Lions play on at the Silverdome. Yet throughout his pro career, Sanders has actually averaged more yards per carry on grass than on artificial turf. He has also rushed for more yards per carry away from home than at the Silverdome.

Sanders had second thoughts about putting on this Detroit Lions' uniform. His new team had just switched to a run-and-shoot offense.

be better off avoiding the Lions. Maybe he could force them to trade him to a more promising team that could better use his talents.

But Sanders had made a career out of proving people wrong. He saw the Lions' passing obsession as a kind of slap in the face. The run-and-shoot seemed to belittle the importance of running backs. "I wanted to change their attitude and make them respect me."[5]

When Sanders first arrived in Detroit to visit with the Lions, Coach Fontes prepared to give him the royal treatment. He sent a limousine to the airport to fetch the college player of the year. Barry immediately let the Lions know that he did not believe in special treatment. He refused the limousine. Sanders insisted on riding in the team van like the lower-round draft choices.[6]

Humble though he was, Barry knew what his skills were worth to pro football teams. He refused to sign a contract that did not pay him what he thought he was worth. He was also concerned that African Americans were thought of as athletes only. He knew how hard it was for blacks to get into some professional fields. To help with that problem, he hired black lawyers and agents to negotiate his contract for him.

While contract talks dragged on, Sanders made

the final step in his commitment to his religious beliefs. That summer he attended a Christian conference in Phoenix. "I saw how hypocritical I had been and that I had to . . . get straight with God. I was baptized while I was in junior high but I really didn't know what it meant."[7] Now that Sanders knew what it meant, he was determined to build his life around his Christian beliefs.

When he finally signed his contract with the Lions, Sanders put his money where his mouth was. One of the first checks that he wrote with his signing bonus of $2 million was made out to Paradise Baptist Church in Wichita. Sanders wrote the check for $200,000. That followed the principle of the Bible calling for giving a tenth of his income to the Lord.

Assistant Pastor Reverend Michael Frost was "awestruck" when he learned of the gift. "Barry's been brought up to give," he said. "I expected him to do something. But nothing of this magnitude."[8]

When he joined the Lions, Sanders became active in leading a weekly Bible study. He also helped arrange Sunday morning services. He remained quiet and modest and did not force beliefs on other people. He even enjoyed teasing some of his teammates. At first he pretended to be upset at some of the earthy language they used.

Sanders, running his pass route, knew that the Lions' offense would require him to get more involved in catching passes.

But there was never any mistaking what Sanders believed and what he valued. Rodney Peete, the Heisman Trophy runner-up to Sanders, joined the Lions at the same time as Barry. "When Barry says something, he means it," Peete said. "He's straightforward and I think, in that way, a lot of guys respect him."[9]

As for his worth on the football field, Sanders was prepared to let his actions do all the talking.

Chapter 5

Rookie

When they selected Barry Sanders with their first-round draft choice, the Detroit Lions were hoping that lightning would strike for the third time. In 1970 the Lions had drafted a Heisman Trophy-winning fullback from the University of Oklahoma on the first round. This player, Steve Owens, powered the Lions offense for several years. In 1971, Owens rushed for 1,035 yards. That was the first time a Lion back had ever broken the 1,000-yard mark for a season.

In 1980, the Lions went back to that formula. They spent their first-round draft choice on running back Billy Sims, the Heisman Trophy winner from the University of Oklahoma. Sims ran wild in his rookie season and jolted a nearly dead franchise back to life. The slashing speedster raced for 1,303 yards to set a new Detroit rookie record. In 1982 and

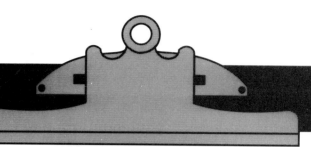

STATS

The Detroit Lions found a good thing in Heisman Trophy winners from Oklahoma universities, and they kept going back to the well. Billy Sims and Sanders rushed comparably in their rookie seasons while Steve Owens was slowed by injury:

Rookie Season Rushing Stats					
PLAYER	YEAR	ATTEMPTS	YARDS	AVG GAIN	TD
Owens	1970	36	122	3.4	2
Sims	1980	313	1,303	4.2	13
Sanders	1989	280	1,470	5.3	14

Career Rushing Stats				
PLAYER	ATTEMPTS	YARDS	AVG GAIN	TD
Owens	635	2,451	3.9	20
Sims	1,131	5,106	4.5	42
Sanders*	1,183	5,674	4.8	52

*through 1992

1983, he powered them into the play offs—a rare treat for Lions' fans. Sims career was cut short due to knee injuries. But in his four seasons, Sims set a Detroit career rushing record of 5,106 yards. He also claimed the team's single-season touchdown record of 16.

Now Detroit was trying again with another Heisman Trophy-winning runner from an Oklahoma school. Sanders, though, faced a mountain of obstacles as he entered his rookie year. Although he had built himself up to 200 pounds, Sanders was slightly smaller than Sims and much smaller than Owens had been. His new team was dedicated to the Silver Stretch passing offense. Coaches had designed few running plays to suit Barry's skills. The offense had no proven quarterback to direct it. In fact, rookie Rodney Peete, a sixth-round draft choice, was taking over the starting role. The team had no star receivers to take the pressure off Sanders. Except for tackle Lomas Brown, the offensive line of the Lions was unsettled. No Detroit back had been able to gain as much as 100 yards in a game during the past two seasons. New linemen were being shuffled in and out of the lineup in a search for decent blocking.

To make matters worse, Sanders did not sign his contract until two days before the first game of the season. That caused him to miss all of training camp, as well as the exhibition games. The team started the regular season with no idea of what Sanders could do for them.

Sanders' long holdout had left him hopelessly behind in trying to learn the Detroit plays. He could only sit on the bench as the Lions opened their season at home against the Phoenix Cardinals. In the third period, though, Detroit decided to give their rookie a brief trial. The Silverdome crowd buzzed as Barry entered the game. The Lions called a simple off-tackle play for him. Sanders took the hand-off and ran toward the tackle spot. He spotted an opening to the outside. He cut, broke toward the sidelines, and turned up field. With the crowd roaring in delight, Sanders galloped for 18 yards before he was stopped.

That spurt so fired up the Detroit offense that the coaches left Sanders in the game. Because of Barry's limited knowledge of the play book, the coaches had to keep calling basically the same play every time he carried the ball. Although the Lions were not fooling anybody, the Cardinals could not stop Sanders. The rookie moved the ball downfield on four carries and burst into the end zone for the score.

Running variations of that one play, Sanders carried the ball nine times in the second half for 71 yards. That averaged out to nearly eight yards per

Sanders looks for an escape as the Cardinals close in.

carry. Barry's performance sparked a Lions' comeback that fell just short. Phoenix won the game by a score of 16–13.[1]

The next Sunday Sanders showed the rugged New York Giants just how much he had learned in one week. He surprised them by jumping into the Lions' complicated passing attack. The back who seldom caught the ball at Oklahoma State burned the Giants for 96 yards on six receptions in Detroit's loss to New York. Barry also ran the ball well, with 57 yards in 12 carries and one touchdown in a losing cause.

Sanders had to take on another of pro football's top defenses the following week when the Lions battled the Chicago Bears. Sanders stunned the Bears. He darted through small cracks in the line and ripped through tacklers. In the first half alone, Barry gained 108 yards on 14 carries. He added 12 more yards in the third quarter before he was forced out of the game with a hip injury. With Sanders out of the way, Chicago then coasted to a 47–27 win.

Barry tried to play against Pittsburgh despite the painful hip. But after being smothered on five straight carries, he headed back to the bench. In the next game, although still bothered by the hip problem, Sanders slipped through Minnesota Viking tacklers time and again to gain 99 yards. The Vikings' coach Jerry Burns was baffled by Barry's ability to

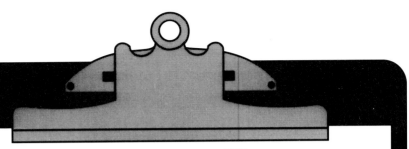

STATS

Most of the top 10 rushers in NFL history have broken into the NFL with a bang. As a rookie, Sanders more than held his own in this group:

Rookie Rushing Performances					
PLAYER	TEAM	ATT	YDS	AVG YDS	TD
Eric Dickerson	Rams	390	1,808	4.6	18
Ottis Anderson	Cardinals	331	1,605	4.8	8
BARRY SANDERS	Lions	280	1,470	5.3	14
Earl Campbell	Oilers	302	1,450	4.8	13
Franco Harris	Steelers	188	1,055	5.6	10
Tony Dorsett	Cowboys	208	1,007	4.8	12
Jim Brown	Browns	202	942	4.7	9
John Riggins	Jets	180	769	4.3	1
Marcus Allen	Raiders	160	697	4.4	11
O. J. Simpson	Bills	181	697	3.9	2
Walter Payton	Bears	196	679	3.5	7

wriggle free from defenders. He asked the game officials to inspect Barry's uniform to see if he was cheating. Burns wondered if Sanders had sprayed himself with silicone to prevent tacklers from getting a grip on him. The officials, of course, found nothing.[2] The complaint amused the Lions. Anyone who knew Sanders would know that Barry was probably the last person in the NFL who would even think of cheating.

Sanders took the next week off so that his injuries could heal. Then he charged back into action with a vengeance against the Green Bay Packers. In the first half, he put in an entire game's work with 123 yards on 19 carries. Barry continued to slice up the Packers in the second half, finishing with 184 yards on 30 carries. His heroic effort fell just short, though. Green Bay squeaked out a 23–20 win in overtime.

By this time, Sanders had finally put to rest those questions about size that had dogged him ever since he first put on shoulder pads. His 184 yards in a game proved he could run the ball against anyone. He had shown that he could carry the ball 30 times against an NFL defense and keep bouncing to his feet ready for more. That erased all doubts about his ability to take a beating.

As observers took a closer look at Sanders, they

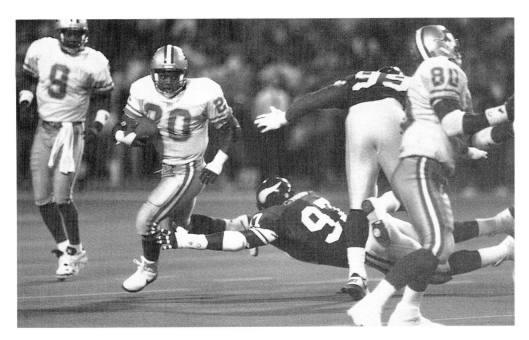

Barry shows the form that had the Vikings wondering if he sprayed something slippery on his uniform as he escapes the grasp of Minnesota's Henry Thomas.

noticed that he was not so small after all. Sure, he was short. Sanders barely stretched the tape to five feet eight inches. But he was powerfully built, especially in the legs. His thighs looked as though they belonged to a beefy offensive lineman. Measuring 31 inches around, they were thicker than many people's waists!

The way Sanders churned those battering-ram legs reminded many football fans of Walter Payton. Recently retired, Payton was the NFL's all-time leader in rushing yardage. After watching Sanders shred Payton's former team, the Chicago Bears, the great ex-running back was more than impressed. "I'm not sure I was that good," Payton admitted.[3]

He may have been remembering a play that had Detroit's offensive coordinator, Mouse Davis, shaking his head in disbelief. The play that had Davis raving was not a long run or a touchdown but a two-yard loss! No sooner did Sanders get the hand-off than the Bears surrounded him in the backfield. As Davis described it, Sanders "spun, went down into a kind of one-legged squat, jumped out and made a guy miss him." Davis called it the most spectacular play of the game.[4] Coming from the creator of Detroit's Silver Stretch passing offense that had little use for running backs, this was high praise.

Despite Barry's contributions, though, Detroit

lost far more often than they won. The Lions limped into their November rematch with the Packers with a 1-8 record. Detroit jumped out to a commanding 24–3 lead at halftime. But the Packers mounted a late threat. Late in the fourth quarter, they closed the gap. The Lions were in danger of going down to another heartbreaking defeat.

Up to this point in the game, Sanders had contributed little. The Packers had remembered what Sanders had done to them in their first meeting. This time they ganged up on Barry whenever he got the ball. Sanders had been held to fewer than 30 yards. But with the game on the line and the Lions desperate for a win, Coach Fontes put the game in Barry's hands. "I don't care what you do," he told quarterback Rodney Peete, "just give it to Barry."[5]

Sanders charged into the line again and again. He spun away from tacklers and spurted through cracks in the line. Five straight carries picked up 40 yards and brought the Lions to the Packer 1-yard line. From there Barry scooted in for the score that clinched Detroit's 31–22 victory.

On Thanksgiving Day, Detroit again called on Sanders for the key yards against the Cleveland Browns. Barry romped for 43 yards in a third-quarter drive that set up the winning field goal. For the game,

Sanders feasted on the Browns for 145 yards rushing and 44 yards on pass receptions.

The New Orleans Saints' tough run defense held Sanders to only 72 yards on December 3. But Sanders again provided the margin of victory in a 21–14 win, this time with power rather than quickness. Sanders broke through three Saints linebackers and plowed into the end zone from the three-yard line for a crucial score.

Sanders finished the season in high gear. He scampered for 120 yards and scored twice against the Bears. He dashed for 104 yards against Tampa Bay to break Billy Sims's Detroit rookie rushing mark of 1,303 yards. Finally, he bolted 158 yards against Atlanta, including touchdown jaunts of 25, 17, and 18 yards.

Sanders passed up a chance to capture the NFL rushing crown. But he did lead the National Football Conference (NFC) with 1,470 yards. Honors poured down on him at the season's end. Sanders was voted Rookie of the Year and All-Pro by several groups and was chosen as a starter in the Pro Bowl game. He had climbed the final hurdle in the ladder of sports. Never again would Barry Sanders have to listen to that tired old line about being too small.

Chapter 6

A Marked Man

Sanders started the 1990 season as a marked man. Opposing coaches no longer designed their defenses to stop Detroit's Silver Stretch passing attack. Now they took aim first at Barry Sanders. Even when the Lions were forced into passing situations, such as third down and long yardage, defenses still geared up to stop Sanders.

Despite the added pressure, Barry broke away for at least one long gain in each of the Lions' first seven games. He contributed a 17-yard touchdown run to help the Lions to a 21–14 victory over the Atlanta Falcons. His 22-yard touchdown pass reception sparked the Lions to a 34–27 victory against the Minnesota Vikings. Sanders riddled the Kansas City Chiefs for 90 yards rushing and 135 yards in pass catches in Detroit's sixth game. Barry dazzled the Chiefs' fans in that game by scoring on a 13-yard run and a 47-yard pass reception.

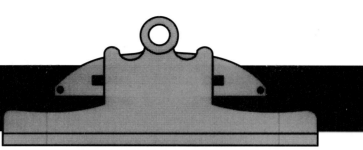

STATS

In recent years Thurman Thomas, Barry's former college teammate, has set the standard for NFL backs in total yardage while playing for Buffalo. Because he has not been as involved as Thomas in the passing game, Sanders has yet to catch Thomas in this department. But he has come close during their four years together in the pros:

Total Yards Gained from Scrimmage				
YEAR	PLAYER	RUSHING YARDS	PASS RECEIVING YARDS	TOTAL YARDS
1989	Thomas	1,244	669	1,913
	Sanders	1,470	282	1,752
1990	Thomas	1,297	532	1,829
	Sanders	1,304	462	1,766
1991	Thomas	1,407	631	2,038
	Sanders	1,548	307	1,855
1992	Thomas	1,487	626	2,113
	Sanders	1,352	225	1,557

But the special attention that Barry attracted from defenses made the yards harder to come by. Sanders did not gain 100 yards in any of his first seven games that year. The Lions' ground game hit rock bottom against the New Orleans Saints in game seven. Sanders seldom made it back to the line of scrimmage. He broke through for one 13-yard gain. But his other 11 carries netted him minus three yards!

Sanders finally exploded against the Washington Redskins. He breezed through the Redskins' defense for huge chunks of yardage as the Lions built up a commanding lead. When Sanders dashed 45 yards into the Redskins' end zone for a 35–15 lead, the game appeared to be won.

At that point, the Lions' fans expected the team to protect its lead by playing it safe and using up the clock with control offense. But Detroit's Silver Stretch was not intended as a ball-control offense. The Lions did not even have extra tight ends to bring in for extra blocking in a power running attack. Although Sanders gained 104 yards for the game and averaged 9.5 yards per carry, he carried the ball only 11 times during the entire game. He scarcely touched the ball at all in the crucial fourth quarter. The Lions' offense sputtered. The defense fell apart. Washington roared back for a 41–38 win.

The frustration continued. Despite averaging over five yards per carry in both games, Sanders ran only 12 times in a 17–7 loss to Minnesota and 11 times in a 20–0 loss to the New York Giants. Detroit's record plunged to 3–7. For the second straight year, Detroit fell out of play-off contention early.

The Lions realized they had to get Sanders more involved in their offense. They called on Barry to carry the ball 23 times against the Denver Broncos. Sanders responded by breaking loose for 147 rushing yards, plus a 35-yard touchdown pass reception. Then, in front of a national television audience, Barry dazzled the Los Angeles Raiders. He scored two touchdowns and piled up 176 yards in 25 carries. That put him over 1,000 yards for the second straight season.

The Lions took on the Packers in a late-season game that meant little to either team. The meaningless contest was being played on a frozen field and in frigid temperatures. Under those conditions, fans could hardly have expected a rousing effort from the players. But Sanders always came to play. He rambled for 135 yards in just 19 carries. With the game on the line in the final minutes, Sanders dashed six yards for the touchdown that gave Detroit a 24–17 win.

Sanders finished the season poorly at Seattle. He carried the ball only 9 times for 23 yards. But that gave him 1,304 yards for the season, which was enough to earn the NFL rushing title that he had missed the previous year. Barry also tied Billy Sims's Detroit record for touchdowns with 16. Again Sanders was named All-Pro and selected to start in the Pro Bowl game.

Throughout his success, Sanders remained quiet and humble. He was determined to be a good role model for youngsters. "I always wanted to be a seed in good ground," he said.[1] Barry wore no flashy jewelry or clothes—he was far more interested in what is inside a person than what a person wears on the outside. "I concentrate on what I should be, not on what others think I should be," he has said.[2]

Sanders continued to credit his offensive linemen for his success. He showed respect for his opponents and never called attention to himself. Barry refused to taunt defenders. He would not dance or celebrate or make any sort of show after his scores. He simply handed the ball to one of the officials and trotted back to the sideline. Although confident about his abilities, Sanders shied away from making predictions about his career. When told that he was a good bet to top Eric Dickerson's record of 2,105 yards in a season, Sanders just shrugged. "Things never turn out the way people expect them to," he said.[3]

Despite his efforts to avoid the spotlight, Sanders had won the admiration of fans, teammates,

FACT

Sanders tries to make sure that his offensive linemen get at least some of the recognition they deserve. Barry's contract calls for a $10,000 bonus for the blockers when he gains more than 1,000 yards in a season. The following Lions led the way for Barry in 1991, his best season:

NAME	POSITION	HEIGHT	WEIGHT
Erick Andolsek	Guard	6'2"	286
Lomas Brown	Tackle	6'4"	287
Ken Dallafior	Guard-Tackle	6'4"	279
Eric Sanders	Tackle	6'7"	286
Kevin Glover	Center	6'2"	282
Mike Utley	Guard	6'6"	300
Scott Conover	Guard	6'4"	276
Roman Fortin	Tackle	6'5"	290
Shawn Bouwers	Guard	6'4"	290

coaches, and opposing players. Kansas City Chiefs' head coach Marty Schottenheimer was asked to compare some of the best running backs in the league. "Let's get this straight right now," said Schottenheimer. "Barry Sanders is in a class all by himself. There's Barry Sanders, then everybody else."[4]

Those who had attempted to tackle Sanders tried to put a finger on exactly what made him so tough to stop. Some of them talked about his explosive start and the power in his thick legs. Others such as Green Bay safety Tiger Greene marveled at Sanders' "unbelievable sense of balance."[5] But most singled out his quickness and his ability to shift direction. Sanders rarely went where tacklers thought he was going. He rarely turned out to be where they thought he was headed. He could start and stop so fast that he had defenders flying out of their shoes trying to stay with him.

Recently retired Chicago Bear linebacker Mike Singletary was considered one of the surest tacklers in football. When asked how you go about stopping Sanders, Singletary said that "first, you have to find him." Sanders was the type of guy, Singletary said, who made you pay for getting too aggressive. "If you try to blast him, chances are he'll spin out of it and you'll end up looking silly."[6]

Green Bay linebacker Brian Noble talked about how low to the ground Sanders ran and how difficult he was to pin down. "You never get *the* shot at him," said Noble. "He's not there anymore."[7]

Pittsburgh defensive coordinator Dave Brazil agreed. "Barry Sanders is the hardest guy to tackle that I've seen in this league in a long time. You can't get a piece of him."[8] Broadcaster and former pro coach Hank Stram cited the same quality. Sanders, said Stram, "never absorbs the full thrust of a hit. Basically, he's unstoppable."[9]

Most pro defensive players study films to figure out a way to stop opposing players. Minnesota Viking linebacker Jack Del Rio decided that was a waste of time with Sanders. "You can't prepare for the things he does," said Del Rio.[10]

Sanders, like every other player, had his faults. He was still learning how to block blitzing linebackers on pass plays. He needed to be more patient. Sometimes he would outrun his linemen before they had a chance to throw a block for him. Sanders could also be *too* relaxed for his own good at times. He fell asleep so easily that he had difficulty preparing for opponents. No sooner would the lights go out for a Lions' film-studying session than Sanders would start to doze.

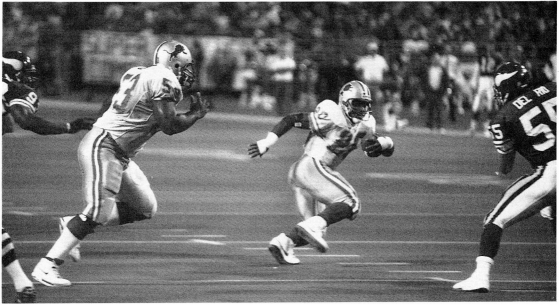

Changing direction at high speed, the long-striding Sanders shows Jack Del Rio (55) a few new moves.

But his teammates were more than willing to overlook such minor faults. To most of them, the quiet Sanders was an inspiration to do better. All-Pro nose tackle Jerry Ball summed up Sanders' influence on his teammates by saying, "In his work ethic, character, discipline, in every way, he sets a standard for everyone on this team."[11]

In the emotional roller coaster that the Lions were about to ride in the next two years, Sanders' steady influence would prove especially valuable.

Despite Barry's spectacular efforts, the Detroit Lions appeared to be going nowhere. Their 6–10 finish in 1990 was a step backward from the 7–9 mark of the year before. Football observers saw little improvement on the horizon. Young quarterbacks Rodney Peete and Andre Ware still needed time to develop. Detroit had no big-play wide receivers. Even with Sanders and an improving offensive line, Detroit could not mount a ball-control offense to protect a lead. They had trouble picking up a tough yard on crucial short-yardage situations.

The Lion defense seemed as flimsy as ever. In 1990, they had given up 413 points, an average of more than 25 points per game. One major preseason publication commented on the Lions' dismal

Sanders kept his occasional frustrations with his role under wraps.

prospects. "The 1991 Season appears to be yet another step in the rebuilding process," it concluded.[12]

By this time, Coach Fontes had become frustrated with the Silver Stretch offense. He worried that Sanders' talents were being wasted in such a scheme. Fontes decided to alter the Silver Stretch into a more balanced offense.

Sanders welcomed the change. He had not complained about the way he had been used in the past. But he had been frustrated with the type of plays he had been asked to run. Nearly all the Lions' running plays had sent Sanders charging into the line where the openings were small and there was little room to maneuver. "I'm an open field runner," Barry noted, "and we didn't have any pitch plays."[13] Detroit's new offense for 1991 included plays more suited to Barry's skills.

Sanders had somehow led the NFL in rushing even in an offense that cramped his style. Lion fans looked forward to seeing what he could do now that he was the center of the team's offense.

Chapter 7

Thumbs Up Season

The 1991 season started off on a bad note. Sanders, who had survived a bruising schedule almost injury free in 1990, hurt his ribs in an exhibition game against the Kansas City Chiefs. But Sanders had healed well enough that he played for a limited time in the Lions' final preseason game. Sanders traveled with the team to Washington's RFK Stadium, expecting to play in the season opener against the Redskins. "I was sure I was going to play," remembers Sanders. "The whole team thought so."[1] In fact the Lions were itching to try out their new offense that was designed especially for their All-Pro running back.

Unfortunately, Sanders' ribs felt sore during the pregame warm-ups. He tried stretching exercises to get them loose, but nothing worked. Just minutes before the game started, the Lions learned that their star would not play. The Redskins battered the Lions from start to finish. Unable to generate any offense without Sanders, Detroit stumbled to a humiliating 45–0 loss.

The disastrous defeat discouraged Detroit's fans. Nothing seemed to have changed. The Lions appeared to be well on their way to yet another losing season. Fans and sportswriters wasted no time in tearing into the Lions for their sad performance against Washington. They criticized Sanders for not playing. Some thought that his injury was not as bad as he claimed and that Barry should have played.

Sanders, who usually paid little attention to the press, was stung. Worse yet, he worried that he had let down his teammates. "I'm sure a lot of guys were upset," he admitted. He wondered if they still respected him or if they questioned his courage the way some fans were doing.[2]

Sanders could do nothing about the past. But he was determined to make the critics eat their words in the Lions' second game. The Green Bay Packers, however, were tired of Sanders running all over them. They had worked extra hard to design their defense to stop him. Barry eked out only 42 yards in 18 attempts and caught 2 passes for zero yards. In order to swarm after Sanders, though, the Packers

Sanders takes on a less glamorous role to help the team. Here he blocks a 265-pound defensive tackle.

had to weaken their pass defense. Detroit won the game, 25–14. Barry's one small success in the game was a short touchdown run.

Sanders finally answered his critics in game three. The coaches kept calling his number, and Barry kept running at the Miami Dolphins. Sanders finished the game with a pro career-high of 32 carries, good for 143 yards.

Near the end of the contest, Detroit clung to a 17–13 lead. They faced a critical third-and-two situation. In the past seasons, the Lions had run into a brick wall in these short-yardage situations. This time they handed off to Sanders, who was hit almost immediately by Dolphin defenders. Sanders showed no weariness from his exhausting day's work. He kept his balance, struggled, and lunged until he got the first down. That run iced a hard-fought 17–13 win.

Both the offense and the defense had played well against a tough opponent. The Lions had shown a toughness that had not been there in past seasons. Suddenly a team that had been written off after their opening-day fiasco bubbled with confidence. Some of the Lions spoke of that Washington drubbing as their "wake-up" call for the season. They charged into Indianapolis and thrashed the Colts, 24–3. Sanders ran wild against Indianapolis for 179 yards on 30 carries, including two touchdowns.

Detroit stretched its winning streak to four games with a 31–3 romp over the Tampa Bay Buccaneers. Sanders provided most of the offensive fireworks with 160 yards on 27 carries and three touchdowns. He capped the victory by breaking through the Tampa front line and outsprinting the defensive backs on a 69-yard touchdown run.

Detroit's winning streak appeared to be stopped cold when they played their tough Central Division rival, the Minnesota Vikings. The Vikings stuffed Detroit's running game. They held Sanders to 47 yards on 15 carries through the first three quarters. The Lions tried to outsmart the Vikings by throwing more passes to Sanders than they ever had before. But nothing worked. With eight minutes left in the game, the Lions trailed, 20–3.

Suddenly Sanders and his teammates caught fire. The Lions scored a touchdown. They recovered an onside kick. As the Silverdome fans roared their approval, Sanders began slicing through the Viking defenders. Detroit scored again to make it 20–17.

The rally inspired the Lion defenders, who stopped the Vikings on their next series. Detroit got the ball back again hoping to move close enough to kick a tying field goal before time ran out.

The Lions raced upfield so quickly that they reached the Vikings' 15-yard line with 43 seconds remaining in the game. They were easily within field goal range. The Lions could run a few safe plays to get even closer. Perhaps they could even get into the end zone to win the game. As the fans chanted, "BARR-REE! BARR-REE," Sanders took a hand-off from Rodney Peete. He waded into a sprawling jumble of blockers and defenders.

Just when it appeared he had been stopped, Sanders flew out of the pile as if shot from a cannon. He raced past Viking tacklers and sprinted for the goal line. Two Viking defensive backs, Reggie Rutland and Joey Browner, hemmed Sanders in before he could get there. Sanders faked, dodged, and twisted as the two defenders tried to stay with him. Finally, Sanders dove low to the ground through the defenders. As he landed, he stretched the ball over the goal line to complete Detroit's remarkable comeback.[3] The Lions' 24–20 victory gave them a 5–1 mark. For the first time, football fans began to take the Lions seriously as title contenders.

Neither Sanders nor the Lions, however, were able to keep up the incredible pace they had started. The 49ers smashed the Lions by a 35–3 score as Sanders gained only 27 yards. The Lions recovered to knock off the Dallas Cowboys. But they then suffered a stinging defeat at the hands of the Chicago Bears, their main rival for the divisional crown. Sanders seemed to be bogged down in a slump. The Bears game marked the third contest in a row in which he had failed to rush for more than 63 yards and had been shut out of the end zone.

Sanders regained his form against Tampa Bay with 118 rushing yards and two touchdowns. But the rest of the team was still stumbling. The lowly Bucs breezed to a 30–21 victory, dropping the Lions to a 6-4 mark.

Detroit took on the Los Angeles Rams knowing that another loss would probably knock the team out of their division championship. In a hard-fought defensive struggle, the Lions claimed a 21–10 victory. Never before had Sanders run the ball so often with so little success. He carried 26 times against the Rams for only 57 yards.

But none of the Lions were thinking about Barry's problems. Nor were they celebrating their victory. Instead, they were somberly replaying a tragic incident that had struck down their teammate, Mike Utley. Utley, a powerful six-foot, six-inch 300-pounder had developed into a fine offensive guard. The third-year man from Washington State had come to the Lions along with Sanders in the 1989 draft. He had been a great help in clearing the way for Sanders' runs. But late in the game, Utley was blocking the Rams' Tracy Rocker on a pass play when disaster struck. Rocker pushed off Utley's shoulder just as the guard lunged forward to maintain his block. Utley tumbled forward and landed on his head.

The Silverdome fell silent as Utley lay motionless on the field. Team doctors carefully placed him

Bonded together by tragedy, the Lions became a close-knit unit. Sanders and tackle Lomas Brown offer each other support.

on a stretcher and carried him off the field. There was no doubt that Utley had been seriously injured. Doctors soon determined that he had fractured a vertebra in his neck and had injured his spinal cord. But as he was carted off the field, Utley found he could still move a thumb. Bravely, he gave the thumbs-up sign to his teammates and fans.

All of the Lions were shaken by the terrible accident and the loss of a teammate. But they tried to take heart from Utley's courage. The Lions decided to dedicate the rest of their season to him. When they dressed for their next game, a rematch with the Vikings, each of the Lions wore a special T-shirt under his uniform. The shirt had a picture of an upraised thumb on the front and Utley's uniform number 60 on the back.

"Because of this week's experience, we felt obliged to go out and do our best," Barry Sanders explained.[4] But no one knew exactly how the emotional stress would affect the team.

Sanders provided the answer by picking up where he had left off against the Vikings in their last thrilling game. He dodged around and dashed through the Vikings on a 17-yard touchdown run early in the game. According to Coach Fontes, "After the first touchdown, I put my arm around him and said that was the best."

A familiar nightmare for the Minnesota Vikings: Sanders breaks through for another long gain.

FACT

On November 23, 1950, veteran running back Bob "Hunch" Hoernschemeyer set a single-game rushing record for the Detroit Lions when he raced for 198 yards. Two games later, second-year man Cloyce Box set a team record with four touchdowns in a single game. Both records went untouched for more than 40 years. Sanders broke Hoernschemeyer's mark and tied Box's in one spectacular game against the Vikings in 1991.

Barry's only response was to come back with a stunning 47-yard touchdown jaunt. "After the second touchdown," said Fontes, "I told him that was even better."

But Sanders had barely begun. Sanders scored a third touchdown on a nifty four-yard effort that Fontes described as "the best of them all."[5] Sanders just smiled. Then he went out and scored his fourth touchdown, this one from nine yards out. By the time Sanders was through demolishing the Vikings, he had racked up a Lions' record of 220 yards rushing on 23 carries. One of Barry's blockers called the performance, "poetry in motion."[6]

The victory boosted the Lions' record to 8–4. For the first time in nearly a decade, they were seriously fighting for their divisional championship. Detroit trailed Chicago by one game going into their Thanksgiving Day showdown against the Bears. Sanders was held in check by the Bears' defense in this game. But the Lions' defense played even better. Detroit won, 16–6.

Sanders then led the way against the New York Jets with touchdown runs of 14 and 51 yards in a 34–20 victory. He ground out 85 yards in 27 carries on a frozen field as Detroit kept their streak alive with a 21–17 win at Green Bay. Finally, he picked up 108 yards rushing and 53 yards in receptions to spark Detroit to a 17–14 win in overtime against Thurman Thomas's team, the Buffalo Bills. The win, coupled with Chicago's loss in their final game, gave Detroit the Central Division title.

Sanders won the NFL touchdown title with a club record of 17. His 1,548 rushing yards also broke his old Detroit mark. Sanders had also led the NFL in rushing going into the Buffalo game. But the Dallas Cowboys' Emmitt Smith racked up 160 yards in 30 carries in his final game to nose out Barry with 1,563 yards to Barry's 1,548.

As luck would have it, the play-off schedule pitted Emmitt Smith and the Cowboys against the Lions. The game was billed as a showdown between the game's top runners. Sanders would get his chance for revenge on the man who had stolen his rushing title on the final day of the season.

The Cowboys were convinced that Detroit could not pass against them. Rodney Peete was injured. Detroit was forced to use inexperienced Erik Kramer at quarterback. Believing that the Lions would be forced to rely heavily on Sanders for offense, the Cowboys stacked their defense near the line of scrimmage.

The Lions, however, had a surprise for the Cowboys when the game opened on January 5, 1992. They simply used Barry as a decoy. Kramer fired

Detroit's redesigned offense gave Sanders something he had sorely missed in his early years—an occasional lead blocker operating out of the backfield.

pass after pass downfield into a wide-open Dallas secondary.

Dallas had gambled so heavily on stopping Sanders that they could not adjust to the unexpected aerial attack. Sanders carried the ball only four times in the first half. Meanwhile, Kramer completed 18 of 22 passes in leading the Lions to a 17–6 first half lead.

At halftime Coach Fontes approached Sanders. "I told him we were going to stick with what we were doing," Fontes said. A star with a bigger ego or a more self-centered nature might have been fuming. This was Barry's first play-off game. It was his chance to show he was really better than Emmitt Smith. Yet his team was not giving him the ball.

But Barry just shrugged and said, "Fine."[7] Sanders was not interested in personal statistics; he wanted to help the team win. Detroit continued to shred the Cowboys. Kramer passed the Lions to a 31–6 lead late in the game. At that point, Barry found a way to show the Cowboys what he could do. He charged into a mass of Dallas defenders on a routine running play. While the Cowboys struggled to get him to the ground, Barry kept those thick legs churning. Suddenly, he popped out the other end of the pile like a train breaking out of a tunnel. He sprinted all the way to the end zone 47 yards away to seal Detroit's stunning 38–6 win.

The Lions eagerly awaited their clash with the Washington Redskins for the NFC championship. They had been embarrassed 45–0 the last time they had played Washington. But the Lions reminded fans that Sanders had not played in that game. With their star back in action, this game would be different.

Unfortunately, it was more of the same. Washington forced two quick turnovers to jump out to a 10–0 lead. As the Lions fell farther behind, they were forced to pass the ball in an attempt to score quickly. Barry rushed only 11 times for 44 yards as the Redskins won, 41–10.

The Lions were disappointed with the final

game. But they looked back on their roller-coaster season with satisfaction. Inspired by Mike Utley's courage and Barry Sanders' record-breaking performance, they had come a long way in one year. Perhaps the Detroit Lions were on their way to the top at last.

Chapter 8

Keeping His Balance

The Lions had withstood the shock of losing Mike Utley in 1991. Out of that tragedy, they had forged a tremendous team spirit that had carried them to the brink of the NFC championship. Unfortunately, the Utley accident proved to be only the beginning of a series of terrible breaks that plagued the Lions.

During the summer of 1992, the Lions' offensive line suffered another tragedy. Guard Erick Andolsek was killed at home when a car ran off the road and struck him. Assistant coach Len Fontes, the head coach's brother, died suddenly of a heart attack that same summer. Injuries racked the offensive line in the preseason. Before long only Lomas Brown remained from the starting 1991 unit. Wayne Fontes later complained that he had never seen a one-year stretch of misfortune like this in his life.

The Lions weathered these repeated losses as best they could. They prepared to face a tough test in their opening game of the season—against the Chicago Bears. The teams waged a close, hard-fought battle into the second half. With the score tied at 10–10, Sanders almost single-handedly took control. He took a hand-off and hunted for an opening as the Bear defenders poured through the weakened Detroit blocking. Sanders pulled out of the grasp of two Bear linebackers who thought they had him tackled. He skittered like a waterbug, charged like a bull, and sprinted like a deer. He reached the end zone 43 yards away for the score that put Detroit ahead, 17–10.

Chicago regained the lead in the fourth quarter. But Detroit struck back with a touchdown pass with just over a minute left in the game. The Bears now trailed 24–20. A field goal would do them no good. They needed to score a touchdown. After running a kickoff back to their 26, the Bears were 74 yards away from the Lion end zone. Their chances of moving that far in less than a minute were slim.

But Chicago's quarterback Jim Harbaugh got hot. He guided his team quickly into Detroit territory. Desperate to hold onto their victory, the Lions' defense finally stiffened just outside their goal line. Chicago faced a fourth down on the Lion six-yard line with only five seconds remaining. On the final play of the game, Harbaugh fired a pass to Dave Waddle in the end zone. Waddle caught it for Chicago's winning score.

The Lions had been reeling from their long string of disasters. This heartbreaking loss knocked the wind out of the team. As the Lion offensive line sagged under the weight of injuries, Sanders found the going tougher and tougher. Detroit's quarterbacks were unable to pass effectively. Opposing teams could afford to load up their defenses to stop Sanders. Barry took a beating as tacklers overwhelmed his blockers and shut down all his running lanes.

Detroit's season went up in smoke. The Lions, who had set their sights on a championship, quickly fell out of contention.

Barry never gave up or pulled himself out of games. He refused to blame his teammates. His strength, his lightning changes of direction, and his rocket-powered acceleration continued to draw raves from opponents. Late in the season, Sanders broke loose against the Cincinnati Bengals. He entered the game needing only 55 yards to break the Lions' career rushing record of 5,106 yards held by Billy Sims.

Sanders took care of that mark early in the game.

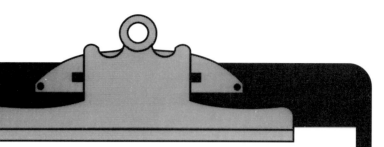

STATS

In his first four seasons, Sanders rushed for more than 150 yards in a game seven times. He does not seem to have a favorite opponent; his seven most productive games have been against seven different teams:

DATE	OPPONENT	ATTS	YARDS	AVG GAIN
11-24-91	Vikings	23	220	9.6
10-29-89	Packers	30	184	6.1
9-22-91	Colts	30	179	5.9
12-10-90	Raiders	25	176	7.0
9-29-91	Buccaneers	27	160	5.9
12-24-89	Falcons	20	158	7.9
11-22-92	Bengals	29	151	5.3

By halftime he had already put some distance between his new record and Sims's old one by gaining over 100 yards. Barry gained 151 yards for the game as he sparked Detroit to a rare 19–13 victory. Bengals' linebacker James Francis marveled at Sanders' performance. "Barry Sanders is one of those guys who shows you something that you'll never see again," he said.[1]

With no hope of making the play-offs, the Lions were playing for little more than pride. Even at this

Overshadowed by other runners in 1992, Sanders sometimes seemed to be a forgotten man.

stage, their respect for Sanders showed. Late in the season, the Lions' offensive linemen said that they had one main goal for the final games. That was to get Barry his 1,000 yards.

Barry's final game of the season summed up the miseries of 1992 in a nutshell. He was working behind his patchwork offensive line against the

Sanders takes a handoff from Rodney Peete and with a powerful burst of acceleration, charges into the line.

San Francisco 49ers, the team with the best record in football. Somehow he managed to gain 104 yards in only 19 carries. Yet he could not crack into the end zone. The rest of the Lions could offer little support. Detroit lost the game 24–6, to finish with a woeful 4-12 mark.

Emmitt Smith had the luxury of playing for the eventual Super Bowl champion Dallas Cowboys. Running behind a powerful, healthy offensive line, Smith again captured the NFL's rushing title. Smith and Pittsburgh's Barry Foster won praise as the NFL's top rushers. Sanders, buried in the ashes of Detroit's miserable season, faded into the background. The man who a year ago had been regarded as the best runner in football was largely ignored.

The fact that Sanders finished second in the NFC in rushing went unnoticed by many fans. Barry achieved the goal set by his linemates. He gained 1,352 yards in 312 carries, more yards than he had gained in 1990, when he had won the rushing title. It was his fourth straight season rushing for over 1,000 yards, and he earned his fourth consecutive start in the Pro Bowl game. Considering the injuries to his blockers and the lack of a passing attack to take the heat off Sanders, many football experts believed that

Barry's "disappointing" 1992 performance was actually his best yet.

The Lions regrouped from their nightmare season. They looked forward to picking up where they had left off in 1991. The first step was to provide blocking for Sanders. With that goal in mind, Detroit signed three veteran free agent linemen before the 1993 season. They added All-Pro pass rusher Pat Swilling to their defense. Meanwhile, they counted on another year's seasoning to help their young players, such as quarterbacks Rodney Peete and Andre Ware, and talented young wide receiver, Herman Moore. They hoped for an end to their rash of injuries.

But the man they counted on the most was still Barry Sanders. Although he already owns many Lions' career rushing records, Sanders was only 25 years old going into the 1993 season. Barring serious injury, Barry could be counted on to lead the Lion attack for many years to come.

Regardless of what happens to the Lions or to Sanders, those who know Barry believe he will keep his balance in the dizzying world of success and money. The quiet man of the Lions has listened well to his parents' advice. He often signs his autographs with a notation from Proverbs

1:7: "The fear of the Lord is the beginning of knowledge."[2]

"He's someone who believes in his ability and he believes in his faith," says Lomas Brown.[3]

Wayne Fontes puts it more simply. "Barry Sanders is not for show; he's for real."[4]

Notes by Chapter

Chapter 1

1. Associated Press report of the 1988 Holiday Bowl (December 31, 1988).

2. Associated Press, December 31, 1988.

3. Tom Felton, "Run, Barry, Run!" *The Life 91 Herald* (January 1993), p. 10.

4. Detroit Lions' media department article "Profile in Faith."

5. Felton.

6. Thomas George, "Carrying Teammates & the Ball," *New York Times Biographical Service* (October 1991), p. 1109.

7. Profile in Faith.

8. Felton.

9. Weinberg, Rick, " Rush Job," *Sport* (August 1991), p. 71

Chapter 2

1. William Nack, "Barry Breaks Away," *Sports Illustrated* (April 10, 1989), p. 24.

2. Felton.

3. Telander, Rich, "Big Hand for a Quiet Man," *Sports Illustrated* (December 12, 1988), p. 47.

4. Personal correspondence from Rev. Paul Gray, Sr. March 1993.

5. Detroit Lions' media department transcript of undated reports from the *Detroit News.*

6. Austin Murphy, "A Lamb Among Lions," *Sports Illustrated* (September 10, 1990), p. 64.

7. Detroit Lions' media department transcript of undated reports from the *Detroit News.*

8. Murphy, Paul Attner, "Barry Sanders—Small Size, But Big Chunks," p. 64.

9. *The Sporting News* (December 19, 1988), p. 12.

10. Rich Reilly, "Quiet Cowboy Riding High," *Sports Illustrated* (October 17, 1988), p. 50.

11. "1988 Heisman Trophy Winner," *Street & Smith's College Football 1989*, p. 12.

Chapter 3

1. Telander, p. 47.

2. Reilly.

3. Reilly.

4. Telander, p. 48.

5. Telander, p. 48.

6. "Profile in Faith."

7. Gray.

8. Telander, p. 47

9. Paul Attner, "Barry Sanders: Small Size, But Big Chunks," *The Sporting News* (December 19, 1988) p. 12.

10. Attner.

11. "Heisman Trophy Winner Sanders Picks Books Over Bush," *Jet* (February 13, 1989), p. 47.

Chapter 4

1. Nack, p. 26.

2. Nack, p. 26.

3. Nack, p. 28.

4. Murphy, p. 64.

5. William Ladson, "Two for the 90s," *Sport* (August 1990), p. 56.

6. George.

7. "Profile in Faith."

8. "Sanders Gives His Church $¼ Million in Tithes," *Jet* (September 25, 1989), p. 51.

9. Felton.

Chapter 5

1. Rick Gosselin, "Backs to the Future," *Street & Smith's Pro Football 1990*, p. 20.

2. Murphy, p. 62.

3. Murphy, p. 62.

4. Murphy, p. 62.

5. Murphy, p. 66.

Chapter 6

1. Detroit Lions media department player profile (1992).
2. "Profile in Faith."
3. Murphy, p. 66.
4. Rick Weinberg, "Rush Job," *Sport* (August 1991), p. 71.
5. Associated Press report (October 30, 1989).
6. Murphy, p. 62.
7. Murphy, p. 62.
8. Gosselin, p. 22.
9. Weinberg.
10. Peter King, "The Players' MVP," *Sports Illustrated* (October 28, 1991), p. 85.
11. George.
12. *Street & Smith's Pro Football 1991*, p. 104.
13. Larry Felson, "On the Offensive," *Street & Smith's Pro Football 91*, p. 8.

Chapter 7

1. George.
2. George.
3. Peter King, "The Roar of the Lions," *Sports Illustrated* (October 14, 1991), p. 32.
4. "No Guarantees," *Sports Illustrated* (December 2, 1991), p. 99.
5. Associated Press reports (November 25, 1991).
6. Associated Press reports (November 25, 1991).
7. Associated Press reports (November 25, 1991).

Chapter 8

1. "Lion's Barry Sanders Rushes For Team Mark," *Jet.* (December 14, 1992), p. 47.
2. Felton.
3. Felton.
4. Murphy, p. 66.

Career Statistics

YEAR	TEAM	G/GS	RUSHING				RECEIVING		
			ATT	YDS	AVG	TD	REC	YDS	TD
1989	Detroit	15	280	1,470	5.3	14	24	282	0
1990	Detroit	16	255	1,304	5.1	13	36	480	3
1991	Detroit	15	342	1,548	4.5	16	41	307	1
1992	Detroit	16	312	1,352	4.3	9	29	225	1
1993	Detroit	11	243	1,115	4.6	3	36	205	0
TOTALS		73	1,432	6,789	4.7	55	166	1,499	5

Where to Write Barry Sanders

Mr. Barry Sanders
c/o Detroit Lions
1200 Featherstone Road
Pontiac, MI 48057

Index